A   L

WILLIAM 〜 SHAKESPEARE

J . D . Sutherland

illustrated by
Laura Cronin

APPLETREE PRESS

First published in 1997 by
The Appletree Press Ltd.
19-21 Alfred Street, Belfast BT2 8DL
Tel: + 44 1232 243074
Fax: + 44 1232 246756

A Life of William Shakespeare
A catalogue record for this book is available from the British
Library.

ISBN 0 - 86281 - 647 - 5

9 8 7 6 5 4 3 2 1

ONTENTS

I

A STRATFORD BOY
Page 5

II

ARRIVAL IN LONDON
Page 13

III

TAMBURLAINE AND AFTER
Page 21

IV

WILLIAM SHAKESPEARE, GENTLEMAN
Page 27

V

THE GLOBE
Page 33

VI

THE MASTER DRAMATIST
Page 41

VII

SHAKESPEARE'S PLAYS
Page 55

16th-century Stratford upon Avon

CHAPTER I
A Stratford Boy

TRADITION has it that William Shakespeare was born on 23 April 1564, the feast day of England's patron, Saint George. He was baptised a few days later on 26 April. In that age of high infant death rates no time was wasted in having a child christened.

William was born in his father's house in Stratford upon Avon, a building that, though much altered, still stands today. It was a good-sized house as his father, John, was one of the chief men of the town. When still a boy, John had come from his father's farm in the countryside and had been apprenticed to a glover. He married Mary Arden, a farmer's daughter, and by the time their son William was four, John had become the town's bailiff, or chief citizen. William was John and Mary's third child, but the first to survive infancy. There would be five to follow him, Gilbert,

Joan, Anne, Richard and Edmund.

All times are times of change, but the mid-sixteenth century was unusually volatile. Elizabeth I became Queen of England in 1558. In retrospect her reign has been portrayed as a golden age, but at the time her citizens were painfully aware of social and religious discord. The Protestant Reformation was still very new and many people regretted the ousting of the Roman Catholic Church. There were doubts as to Elizabeth's legitimacy, and many believed that Queen Mary of Scotland had a stronger claim to England's throne. There was also great uncertainty abroad - France was in turmoil and the mighty empire of Spain was hostile and threatening. And the very globe seemed to be changing as new and exciting horizons were being explored. America had been 'discovered' for sixty years, and adventurers were keenly aware of the rich potential for those who were bold and ruthless enough to take to the seas; part-explorers, part-pirates, part-traders, wholly opportunists.

Stratford itself was a solid, old-fashioned country town. The surrounding farming country was rich, the forests full of game. Numerous prominent and wealthy men lived in the area. They built manor houses and castles and some of them were grand enough to be visited by the Queen on her summer travels. Elizabeth I is known to have stayed with the Earl of Leicester at Kenilworth Castle, Lord Warwick at Warwick Castle and Sir Thomas Lucy at Charlecote Manor, only four miles from Stratford.

Earl of Leicester

As a child, Shakespeare had the freedom of both the town and the countryside. He was aware not only of urban matters - councils, debates, law sessions - but also the life of the farm with all the details of animal husbandry, the rhythm of the seasons, the rivers, the forests and the fields.

From the age of seven, already able to read and

Anne Hathaway's Cottage

write, perhaps taught by William Gilbert, the curate, Shakespeare went to school. His father's status ensured him free education at Stratford's grammar school, under the charge of an Oxford-educated master. School began at 6 a.m. in summer and 7 a.m. in winter, and continued until 5 p.m., with a break to allow the pupils to go home for the mid-day meal. Most of the time was taken up in the teaching of Latin. Discipline was strict and the teaching methods traditional - original thought was discouraged and the curriculum was narrow. Shakespeare's comments on school in his plays are wry at best, as in his portrait of the whining schoolboy: *"With his satchel, And shining morning face, creeping like snail, Unwillingly to school."*

It seems unlikely that William shone as a pupil, but he persevered. The first plays he was introduced to were Latin comedies and later he read Ovid, Virgil and Horace. Ben Jonson's famous claim, that Shakespeare had 'little Latin and less Greek' may have been true as far as Greek was concerned, but not in the case of Latin.

9

In 1576, when William was twelve, John Shakespeare's fortunes suffered a blow and the family's prosperity collapsed. In the small world of Stratford it must certainly have undermined the family's pride. It must also have come as quite a shock for, only a few months before, John had applied for a coat of arms, to be recognised officially as a gentleman, but no more was heard of that for a long time.

As a result some writers suggest that William was unable to complete his schooling. It is known that his expectations to attend the university at Oxford, less than forty miles away, were never realised and it is assumed that he instead had to find work. Just what he did is not certain, but it is very likely that he became a lawyer's clerk. The plays reveal such an intimate knowledge of the language and practice of law, that it could hardly have been gathered without direct experience. However, the same thing has been

10

Anne Hathaway

said about Shakespeare's many nautical references and it has been suggested that at some point, as a young man, he went to sea. In other accounts he served as a foot-soldier in the Earl of Leicester's campaign against the Spanish in the Netherlands.

The youth had time for other activities, too. William was only sixteen when he began a love affair with a woman nine years older, Anne Hathaway, who lived on her father's farm (now known as 'Ann Hathaway's Cottage'), in the village of Shottery. He was only eighteen when she became pregnant by him and a wedding was arranged somewhat hastily for 1 December, 1582. The couple then went to live with Shakespeare's parents in Stratford and six months later a daughter was born, and baptised Susanna. Early in 1585 she was followed by twins, Hamnet and Judith. It may have seemed that William, with his father in decline, and now with a wife and young family to support, was firmly chained to Stratford. But Shakespeare's interests and ambitions were clear and so, around 1587, he set off for London.

11

16th-century London

CHAPTER II

Arrival in London

VARIOUS stories have been fashioned to explain why Shakespeare left Stratford, but none are supported by any real evidence. The tale of his disgrace at being caught poaching deer from Sir Thomas Lucy's estates first appeared more than one hundred years after his death. It is likely that the most obvious explanation is also the correct one. William Shakespeare was a man of exceptional intelligence and foresight. He had ambition and, having chosen a profession, he knew that Stratford was not the place to make his plans happen.

From his earliest years, Shakespeare had seen entertainments and pageants performed. Popular traditions were still strong and every town had parades and dancing on feast days. Strolling players travelled from town to town, performing in stable yards or town markets, and although these primitive companies were mostly formed of musicians and jugglers, there were some who could perform short sketches or enact parts of the old medieval miracle and mystery plays. The typical play of the period was a dramatised Bible story or moral tale which showed how Virtue was rewarded and sins such as Sloth or Pride led to damnation. In his time as bailiff, John Shakespeare would have had to authorise such groups before they could perform in Stratford and as a chief citizen would have occupied a front seat.

The next level of drama was to be found in some schools and the universities, where plays in both Latin and English were performed by the students and masters as private entertainments. Some of the nobility kept their own troupes of professional players, to provide entertainment in the winter evenings, though again they were more likely to be acrobats, musicians and tumblers than actors.

During Shakespeare's lifetime things changed dramatically. The Queen preferred a more intelligent and sustained court entertainment than the 'interluders' of her father's reign could provide. As a result the Earl of Leicester set up a troupe of players to perform to the Queen's tastes. This troupe, and others also supported by the aristocracy went on provincial tours in the summer, and included Stratford on their itinerary. By the time Shakespeare was married, the Queen's, the Earl of Leicester's and the Earl of Worcester's troupes had all performed in Stratford and he had seen the most current productions. The plays themselves were still feeble, melodramatic and moralising, but change was in the air and a dramatic revolution was about to happen.

Elizabeth I

Whatever Shakespeare's previous employment may have been, there is no doubt that once he arrived in London, the young man attached himself to the theatrical life of the capital. With no money, no

15

Strolling Players

experience, and no aristocratic patron, he started at the bottom as a 'hireling', perhaps with the Queen's company, doing everything from performing minor acting roles to helping out as an odd-job man.

London in the sixteenth century was by far the biggest town in England. Most of the population of 200,000 lived packed within the city walls in a maze of narrow streets. A hundred years would pass before the Great Fire ravaged the medieval city. St. Paul's was still a gothic structure with a spire. There was only one bridge over the Thames, London Bridge, an astonishing structure which supported houses and shops built over the river. Just outside the city to the west were the Inns of Court - the law colleges and a centre of intellectual life, and further to the west lay the buildings of Westminster, Whitehall Palace, the Abbey, and the town houses of the nobility.

To anyone arriving from the country, London was a place of indescribable confusion, bustle and excitement. From court society to market porters and tavern drinkers, all displayed a swagger and boldness.

17

London lived noisily and lustily whether it was in politics, trade, warfare or entertainment. Of the latter there was plenty – parades, progressions of costumed dignitaries, displays of the different guilds and livery companies, and the ever-popular public floggings and executions. But it was outside the city walls, in the northern suburb of Shoreditch and across the river in Southwark, that Londoners went to enjoy professional entertainment.

In Shoreditch were two theatres, the Theatre and the Curtain. In Southwark, among the prisons, pleasure gardens and brothels were two places of entertainment - the newly-built Rose Theatre and the Beargarden, which offered bear-baiting and horse-baiting. 'Entertainments' such as these were as popular with the Elizabethans as they had been with the ancient Romans.

The theatre in the time of Elizabeth I, and for a long time after, had a very doubtful social status. Great men like the Earl of Leicester kept actors under their protection, but only as unpaid servants. Those

18

responsible for public order kept a vigilant eye on the playhouses, equally wary of any immorality on stage or in front of it. There was a very strong Puritanical streak in society and frequent campaigns to have the theatres shut down.

As a result, those involved in the theatre were seen to be social rebels or outcasts, living at the fringe of society. No-one of any social standing would countenance a son taking to the theatre, and women were forbidden to perform on stage. The dramatist Christopher Marlowe, whose play *Tamburlaine The Great* was on its first production the talk of London, died in a tavern brawl in 1593. Such was the world that Shakespeare entered, but Shakespeare was no Bohemian. He had a family to support, and an ambition to achieve. He intended to restore the Shakespeare name to its proper dignity in the town of Stratford upon Avon, and he proposed to do this through the theatre and drama.

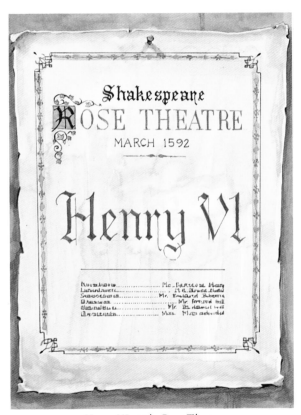

Henry VI at the Rose Theatre

CHAPTER III

Tamburlaine and After

MARLOWE'S *Tamburlaine The Great* was performed by the Admiral's Men at the Rose Theatre in the winter of 1587 and the soaring, resonant imagery of its blank verse opened a great new era for English theatre. For the first time, play-goers heard real dramatic poetry in their own language. Coupled with violent action and an unforgettable leading character, played by the actor Edward Alleyn, *Tamburlaine The Great* was a spectacular success which every dramatist set out to emulate.

The first mention of a play by Shakespeare occurs five years after his arrival in London. Philip Henslowe, manager of the Rose, listed *Henry VI* as a new play in March 1592. However, we know that Shakespeare made his mark some time before that. In

August 1592, the death-bed pamphlet of the writer Robert Greene makes reference to

> *"An upstart Crow, beautified with our feathers, that ... supposes he is as well able to bombast out a blank verse as the best of you ... in his own conceit the only Shake-scene in a countrie."*

Greene had been one of the University Wits whose writing in the 1580s had prepared the way for Marlowe and Shakespeare. Professional jealousy aside, there is some reason for his jibe, because much of Shakespeare's time as an apprentice-writer would undoubtedly have been taken up by improving the text of plays, including Greene's. His attack is notable for another reason too – the publisher of the pamphlet, Henry Chettle, soon after took the almost unheard-of step of printing a public apology to the 'upstart Crow'.

So it seems that by the time *Henry VI* was opening, Shakespeare was already well known. It is likely that he was established at the Rose Theatre both

acting and writing with Lord Strange's company and
working alongside Richard Burbage, Edward Alleyn's
rival as the leading tragic actor of the time.

Unfortunately, that summer a combination of
Puritan pressure, disorderly gatherings at Bankside

and a fresh outbreak of the plague brought about the
closure of the London theatres, and this was repeated
in 1593. After these two disturbed and unrewarding
years, Strange's men became the Lord Chamberlain's;
and since the Lord Chamberlain was the Queen's
Master of the Revels, Shakespeare suddenly found

23

himself part of the most prestigious company in the profession. In summer they played at the Theatre in Shoreditch, in winter at the Cross Keys Inn in the city. By now Shakespeare had been able to purchase a share in the company and was one of the 'adventurers' who bore the risk and shared the profits.

During the plague years it is likely that Shakespeare spent a considerable part of his time in Stratford. He was already in a position to solve his father's money problems (the old man had been unable to leave the house for fear of arrest by his creditors.) Most importantly of all, Shakespeare now

had the time to write. At twenty-eight, a promising and prominent playwright, he was coming to terms with his own talent and his creative energy had moved beyond drama to pure poetry. He was writing sonnets, the fourteen-line poem introduced from Italy by Sir Thomas Wyatt only a few decades earlier, and also his first long poem, *Venus and Adonis*, which he dedicated to the young Earl of Southampton. The poem was printed and published in London in 1593 by his boyhood friend from Stratford, Richard Field. In the next ten years ten editions were issued and this, with his other long poem, *The Rape of Lucrece*, established Shakespeare's name as a major poet. The Sonnets meanwhile, though not printed until 1608, were already being eagerly passed around in hand-written form.

Shakespeare coat of arms

CHAPTER IV

William Shakespeare, Gentleman

*I*N August 1596, tragedy struck the Stratford household. Shakespeare's only son, Hamnet, died at the age of eleven. His father's grief may be seen in these lines from the play he was writing at this time, *King John*:

> *"Grief fills up the room of my absent child,*
> *Lies in his bed, walks up and down with me,*
> *Puts on his pretty looks, repeats his words,*
> *Remembers me of all his gracious parts,*
> *Stuffs out his vacant garments with his form."*

Only shortly before, Shakespeare had renewed his father's application for a coat of arms. The arms were granted later that year, making John Shakespeare and his descendants gentlemen. But in the death of Hamnet, William had lost his own chance to contribute to the furtherance of the family name.

Even when in residence in London, Shakespeare took his position as a family man seriously. There is no evidence to suggest that he played a part in the raffish or dissolute side of the theatre. He did not mix with the street and tavern entertainers or the hangers-on and social drop-outs who associated with them. His London house was located in the parish of St. Helen's, Bishopsgate, a rented accommodation not far from the company's two sites of performance, but it would seem that, despite his long absences, he still saw Stratford as his home.

In 1596 the Lord Chamberlain died, and his son, Lord Hunsdon, became patron of the company. He was later appointed to his father's position and became Lord Chamberlain in 1597. His company found a home in the newly-built Swan Theatre on the south bank and Shakespeare moved lodgings to be closer to it. The Swan is the earliest theatre of which we have a contemporary illustration. The artist, a

Dutchman called Johannes de Witt, claimed it could seat 3,000 people.

On May 4th 1597, just after his 33rd birthday, Shakespeare bought New Place, one of the best houses in Stratford, right in the centre of the town. It cost him £60, a high price, but much of the town had been destroyed by fire and property was expensive. The renaissance of the family was complete. The poet's parents, wife, daughters and brother Richard moved into New Place and Shakespeare's sister Joan and her husband took over the old house on Henley Street. Richard maintained the family business in Stratford; Gilbert had moved to London, where he traded as a haberdasher. The youngest brother, Edmund, also came to London to follow the example of his famous eldest brother and to become an actor.

It has been said that poetic geniuses are unstable, unworldly and dead by the age of thirty-six. If this generalisation has any truth, then William Shakespeare was a notable exception. Far from being unstable, he was a man of balance, who could

Johannes de Witt's sketch of the Swan Theatre

reconcile within himself the contradictions and excesses of humanity. On one level he attended on the Lord Chamberlain and performed before the Queen, choosing to dramatise his country's recent history under the eyes of that suspicious Tudor sovereign and her autocratic government, and showing great political as well as literary dexterity in the process. On another level he was a careful man of business who may have lent money but made sure he got it back, by going to the law if necessary - his sympathy with the despised moneylender Shylock in *The Merchant of Venice* has some basis in experience. Stratford businessmen such as his friend Richard Quiney, borrowed from him and sought to advise him on investments. And finally, far from being dead at the age of thirty-six, his greatest work was still to come.

Interior of the Globe Theatre

CHAPTER V
The Globe

I N 1599 a new theatre, the Globe opened on the South Bank, near the Rose. It was partly constructed from the timber of the Curtain Theatre which was owned by Cuthbert Burbage. The other investors in the Globe were Shakespeare, his fellow actors, Will Kempe and Cuthbert's brother, James. It was a highly self-contained little company and the actor-owners were to do very well out of it financially, especially as their own talents and the scripts of their star writer ensured such a succession of full houses that the owners of the Rose were obliged to move further away.

Purpose-built theatres were still novelties in the sixteenth century. Outside London plays were performed in halls and inn-yards or in natural open-air arenas. Only London had 'real' theatres. When the Globe was built it was by far the most impressive, commodious and well-appointed theatre of the day. Largely based on the galleried layout of the inner yard of Tudor inns but influenced also by the semi-circular amphitheatres of ancient Greece and Rome with tiered seats and an open stage, the theatre was a highly-specialised building for its time.

Although composed of simple elements, its layout was unique. It afforded a raised stage with a gallery above, side entrances and a roof, plus a dressing room for the actors, space to store the few props needed and accommodation for the spectators. As the audience was composed of almost every class of society, the audience area ranged from covered galleries with seats for those of rank to an unroofed area with standing room only, directly in front of the stage, for the common public. The occupants of this area came quickly to be known as the 'groundlings'. The grandest members of the audience were sometimes even seated on the stage itself. The whole building was made of wood and the shape required clever carpentry, but such skills were readily available in a city where wooden ships were built and half-timbered houses were standard. The stage had no front curtain and scenery was kept to a minimum. The same unchanged layout served as the blasted heath in *Macbeth*, the fairy dells of *A Midsummer Night's Dream* and the castle of Elsinore in *Hamlet*. The words and the actions led the audience.

Today the Globe lives again in London, meticulously reconstructed on its Elizabethan plan and dedicated to performing Shakespeare's plays in modern style in an authentic recreation of their original setting.

On the stage, it is likely that Shakespeare played mostly minor roles. It is known however, that his role as an actor was much less important than his position as the company's playwright. Richard Burbage was the principal tragic actor while Kempe was the comic actor of the group. When Kempe sold his share in the company, his place was taken by the accomplished Robert Armin, for whom Shakespeare created such roles as Touchstone in *As You Like It* and the Fool in *King Lear*. Previously the role of the fool was solely that of a noisy intermission from the main plot - a collection of songs, jigs and bawdy remarks - but in Shakespeare's later work the fool assumes a real significance in the action of the play.

Henslowe and Alleyn, impresarios of the Rose, did not take the Globe's assault lying down. In 1600 they established the Fortune theatre in the northern suburb of Finsbury. The Fortune was even bigger than the Globe, but built on a square rather than a round plan. Despite the authorities' efforts to keep down the number of theatres, competition for audiences was intense. There was now a variety of theatres north of the river, including Blackfriars where the 'singing boys' of the Chapel Royal became the new sensation. Plays were still expected to contain elements of music and dance and the boys' voices were infinitely better than the voices of grown men who

were primarily actors rather than trained singers. 'Paul's Boys', from the Cathedral singing school, also performed in public, and plays and musical shows were specially written for them to perform. Despite Shakespeare's tremendous reputation, the Globe was

37

hard hit for a time and was forced to sell some assets. Some texts were sold including *Henry IV Part II* and *Much Ado About Nothing*. However, the magnificent new plays which Shakespeare rapidly wrote - such as *Hamlet* in 1601 - ensured that the crowds did not stay away for long.

As we have seen, Shakespeare was almost a model citizen – prudent in his finances and in his politics, and undoubtedly an entirely loyal subject of Elizabeth I, whose lineage he had celebrated in the historical plays. He must therefore have been horrified by the events of February 1601, when the Globe theatre and his work were dragged into an attempt to overthrow the Queen. One of the chief conspirators was the Earl of Southampton to whom Shakespeare's two long poems had been dedicated. The ring-leader was the Earl of Essex, cousin to the Queen, who hoped to take her place. Essex's supporters paid the Globe's management to change the programme at short notice and put on a performance of *Richard II*, one of Shakespeare's early plays, which deals with the deposition and murder of a King of England. This crude attempt at propaganda warfare merely helped to forewarn the government. Essex's attempt to rouse London against the adored Gloriana was a hopeless failure – less than three weeks later he was beheaded in the Tower of London. Southampton, at first also sentenced to death, had his punishment reduced to life imprisonment.

It was a dangerous moment for the Chamberlain's men, and the agents of the government would certainly have searched for any links they had with the rebels and the rebellion. The Globe, the playwright and the company survived the official scrutiny, but, whether it was a direct effect or not, some critics have detected a darker, deeper and more questioning tone in the plays that come after the events of 1601.

James I

CHAPTER VI

The Master Dramatist

AS Shakespeare's wealth increased, he purchased more property in Stratford. In 1603 he invested in a farming estate to the north of town. He did not intend to live on the estate - it was purely a financial arrangement to secure income from the tenant farmers. Two years later, in 1605, he bought a lease of the corn and hay tithes. This involved an outlay of £440 of his capital against a regular annual income of £60. Shakespeare may have been making his money in London, but his heart and long-term plans were firmly rooted in Stratford.

In March 1603, Queen Elizabeth died, after a reign of forty-four years. Stage plays were forbidden as part of the mourning for the Virgin Queen, and the country anxiously awaited the arrival of her heir, King James VI of Scotland. London's small community of actors' companies was united in fear of the new monarch – after all, they reasoned, James was from Scotland, a country that had embraced a fierce Calvinism which regarded the theatre as diabolical. Luckily though, James loved the stage and when the Lord Chamberlain died later that year, the King himself took over patronage of the Chamberlain's men.

During James's reign, court performances became more frequent, and the period of the Christmas Revels went far beyond the original twelve days of Christmas. In addition, Shakespeare and his colleagues took a step up the social ladder - they now wore royal scarlet liveries and ranked as Grooms of the Chamber.

Later in 1603, Shakespeare moved his London lodgings back into the city proper, to Silver Street, in the parish of St Olave's. He took rooms in the house of Christopher Mountjoy, a wealthy artist-craftsman who supplied the ladies of the court, including the Queen, with fashionable jewelled head-dresses. Not far from his Silver Street rooms was the Mermaid Tavern, the favourite meeting place of poets, wits and intellectuals. The Mermaid Club, as it became known, included John Donne, whose daring and brilliant poems were passed around in manuscript, Ben Jonson, an established playwright, the architect Inigo Jones, who was also Jonson's collaborator as a designer of elaborate masques and tableaux put on to celebrate special events, and two ambitious young playwrights, John Fletcher and Francis Beaumont. Shakespeare is not recorded as having been a member of the Mermaid Club, but it seems most unlikely that he sat gravely at home while the Mermaid Club was in

Gathering at the Mermaid Tavern

session.   Indeed Thomas Fuller recorded in his *Worthies of England* (1662) that Shakespeare and Jonson had many 'wit-combats':

> *"Master Jonson was built far higher in learning; Solid but Slow in his performances. Shakespeare with the English-man of war, lesser in bulk, but lighter in sailing, could turn with all tides, tack about and take advantage of all wind, by the quickness of his Wit and Invention."*

As a coda to the good-natured rivalry that certainly existed between Jonson and Shakespeare, the last record of Shakespeare appearing as an actor is in Jonson's *Sejanus*, which was performed by the King's Men in 1603.   But while Shakespeare's new plays drew full houses, *Sejanus* was a failure with the public.

The accounts of the court revels for the winter of 1604-5 demonstrate clearly how Shakespeare outshone his rivals.   Although there were now three royal companies (Prince Henry's and the Queen's were the others), of the twenty-two plays presented, eleven were performed by the King's men and eight of those were written by Shakespeare.

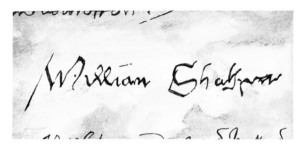

In 1607 Shakespeare's daughter Susanna married a Stratford doctor, John Hall. But not all the family news that year was good: his youngest brother Edmund, who had come to London to become an actor, died during the winter. Nothing is known of Edmund's career, save the bare entry in a burial record: 'Edmund Shakespeare, a player'. Better news came with the birth of Shakespeare's first grandchild, Susanna's daughter Elizabeth, in February 1608. But

46

then, in September 1608, Shakespeare's mother died.

Shortly before his mother's death, Shakespeare had made a further investment in the theatre, along with leading members of the King's men, by taking over the small theatre at Blackfriars. This was an enclosed theatre, unlike the Globe, and therefore much more suited to winter and bad-weather performances. Catering to a wealthier and indeed elite clientele, with no room for groundlings, the Blackfriars encouraged a more intimate style of acting. It was not seen as the right place to perform Shakespeare's plays, and Ben Jonson became the King's men's writer for Blackfriars. At this time too, the aspiring dramatists Beaumont and Fletcher were brought in to extend the company's range of plays and maintain its superiority. Clearly Shakespeare was not a man to harbour professional jealousy or fear of his younger rivals, and the Blackfriars proved an excellent investment.

During this period, London was repeatedly troubled by outbreaks of plague. To try to contain the disease, the magistrates closed the theatres when deaths exceeded thirty a week, which they frequently did. As a result, even the King's men were obliged to go on provincial tours to make money and avoid the pest-ridden capital - and once again they had to sell texts to make ends meet. It is likely that Shakespeare, still writing with as much facility and invention as ever, spent a lot of his time at New Place, his Stratford residence, combining his writing with his country interests.

The Sonnets, which he had been writing for the past twenty years, were published in 1609 with the dedication that has maddened literary sleuths ever since - to the 'onlie begetter' of the poems, 'Mr W. H.' The collection was of great personal importance to Shakespeare. Despite the artificial conventions and mannerisms of the sonnet form, here was a chance to air his own thoughts and feelings, to be himself - Shakespeare's Sonnets are the clearest guide we have to his unique mind.

A year later he took the step which must have been long-planned: instead of living in London and making excursions to Stratford, he based himself in Stratford and travelled to London when necessary.

In April 1612, Shakespeare was called to appear as a witness in a court case. It seems that when Shakespeare lived in Christopher Mountjoy's house, he had been instrumental in arranging a marriage between Mountjoy's daughter, Mary, and Mountjoy's apprentice, Stephen Belott. Shakespeare's former landlord was far from happy with the marriage, and Shakespeare was called as a character witness for the groom.

The Globe on fire

In 1613, Shakespeare finally bought a house in London. It was a substantial residence, the gate house of the old Blackfriars priory, and very near the theatre. Perhaps there were moments when the country cousins and the puritanical tendencies of Stratford were too much for him, and he wanted a place of his own to which he could retreat.

Among thespians, *Macbeth* has always been held to be the 'unlucky' play. But the disaster that struck the Globe Theatre on 29th June 1613, was caused by Shakespeare's newest play, *Henry VIII*, which he had written in collaboration with Fletcher. Among the stage effects were a small cannon and the torches used to fire the guns, which also set fire to the thatched roof. In the resulting blaze the theatre was utterly destroyed. Thankfully, no-one was injured and the invaluable play-books containing the texts were saved. The Globe was to be speedily rebuilt, this time with a tiled roof. However it was around this time that Shakespeare sold his interest in both the Globe and the Blackfriars, ceased to be one of the King's men, and returned to Stratford for good.

He may have suspected he had not many years ahead of him. His younger brothers, Gilbert, Richard, and Edmund were already dead. There have been theories that he was a sick man already, but these have little supporting evidence. Indeed, when Shakespeare made his will in 1615, it proclaimed him to be 'in perfect health and memorie God be praysed'. He also continued to travel regularly between Stratford and London – a two-day journey on horseback and not a trip for the weak or infirm.

In Stratford there was controversy and trouble about the enclosure of common ground by the proprietors. Though Shakespeare did not seek to enclose the common land that he owned, he did not sympathise with the riotous tactics of the protesters. He believed that good fortune came from stability in all things, from the founding powers of the universe down to the petty affairs of men.

Despite a proliferation of cousins, nephews and godchildren, Shakespeare's dynastic aims continued to be frustrated. His daughter Judith married Thomas Quiney, the son of his old Stratford friend, Richard, in 1615. But neither she nor Susanna were to produce a son to survive and bear the Shakespeare coat of arms.

In February 1616, Shakespeare rode to London to see the final performances of the court revels. It was to be his last visit. His daughter Judith told how he came home with a fever after celebrating with Ben Jonson, Michael Drayton, and no doubt other members of the Mermaid Club. He died on his fifty-second birthday and was buried in Stratford's Holy Trinity parish church on 25th April. One of the labours of his retirement had been to prepare the scripts of his plays for publication, but it was not until 1623, a full seven years after his death, that his old friends and colleagues, John Heminge and Henry Condell, published the First Folio of his collected plays.

Mr. WILLIAM

SHAKESPEARES

COMEDIES,
HISTORIES, &
TRAGEDIES,

Published according to the True Originall Copies

LONDON

Printed by Isaac Iaggard, and Ed. Blount. 1623.

First Folio

CHAPTER VII

Shakespeare's Plays

THIS little study concentrates on Shakespeare's life and times and does not attempt to describe the plays. But of course the plays and the life cannot be entirely separated and this chapter sets out to give a short account of Shakespeare's plays as they appeared. By 1592, the year of Robert Greene's sour comment, Shakespeare was probably the author of a number of history plays. His first play (which he largely based on a text by an earlier playwright) *Henry VI Part I*, was quickly followed with *Parts II* and *III* and *Richard III*. He also wrote two comedies, *The Taming of the Shrew* and the *Comedy of Errors*, and *Titus Andronicus*, a tragedy of revenge. Written in the blank verse that Marlowe had made into a flexible and powerful medium, these plays have a tendency to declamation, vivid, but somewhat two-dimensional characterisation and, especially *Titus*

Andronicus, scenes of gore and violence. These are the plays that made his early reputation. The work of the man from Stratford, a common player, became the talk of the town; and London theatre-goers waited with ever-greater anticipation to see what would come next.

In the years between 1594 and 1598 Shakespeare wrote *Two Gentlemen of Verona*, *Love's Labours Lost*, *Romeo and Juliet*, *Richard II*, *A Midsummer Night's Dream*, *King John*, *The Merchant of Venice*, *The Merry Wives of Windsor*, *Henry IV Part 1*, *Henry IV Part 2* and *Much Ado About Nothing*. These plays show a developed maturity: there is more use of dramatic prose, which supports comedy as effectively as it does tragedy and lends a natural touch to verbal fireworks like those which take place between Beatrice and Benedick in *Much Ado About Nothing*. The verse is as rich and allusive as before, but more tightly linked to displaying character and furthering the action. Shakespeare as poet and dramatist was at this stage a complete master of his craft.

There were no professional reviewers or critics

in those days and as a result there is little documentation on how the plays were received. But occasional references from the time show how Shakespeare dominated the scene. One of his rivals noted that the audience were talking 'pure *Romeo and Juliet*'.

When the Globe Theatre opened in 1599, its first production was *Henry V*. *Julius Caesar*, *As You Like It*, *Hamlet*, *Twelfth Night*, *Troilus and Cressida* and *All's Well That Ends Well* followed. Shakespeare appears always to have written with astonishing speed and facility – 'his mind and hand went together,' said his

57

associates Heminge and Condell. By comparison, Ben Jonson, who was now emerging as a rival (much to the relief of the Admiral's Company, who had had no star writer since Marlowe's death), was a laborious, slow and painstaking author.

The accession of King James I of England opened a golden period. The plays of this time, between 1603 and 1608, are mostly of a sombre or tragic cast. They include *Measure for Measure*, *Othello*, *Macbeth*, *Antony and Cleopatra*, *Pericles*, *Coriolanus*, *Timon of Athens* and, perhaps his supreme tragedy, *King Lear*. From 1608, when the King's men were performing both at the open-stage Globe and the closed-in Blackfriars, his approach changed. Like the shrewd actor-manager he was, Shakespeare saw that public taste was changing and he responded to it. There was a demand for tragi-comedy, where a tragic situation is artfully brought to a happy conclusion, and he led it with plays such as *Cymbeline*, *The Winter's Tale*, and *The Tempest*.

The play co-written with Fletcher, *Henry VIII*,

59

was still to come, as was another collaboration, *Cardenio*, whose text did not survive. But most scholars agree that *The Tempest* marks the end of the Shakespeare canon. No-one who has heard or read these elegiac lines in that beautiful, many-layered play can avoid linking them to the playwright himself:

> *"Our revels now are ended. These our actors,*
> *As I foretold you, were all spirits, and*
> *Are melted into air, into thin air;*
> *And, like the baseless fabric of this vision,*
> *The cloud-capp'd towers, the gorgeous palaces,*
> *The solemn temples, the great globe itself,*
> *Yes, all which it inherit, shall dissolve,*
> *And, like this insubstantial pageant faded,*
> *Leave not a rack behind. We are such stuff*
> *As dreams are made on; and our little life*
> *Is rounded with a sleep."*